ABOUT THE AUTHOR

Georgina Wilding was crowned Nottingham's first Young Poet Laureate 2017 – 2019, and went on to accept the prestigious role of Creative Director of Nottingham Poetry Festival until early 2021. In 2015 she set up the poetry publishing house, Mud Press, and in the same year graduated from the University of Nottingham with a first class degree in Creative and Professional Writing.

She spent the first five years of her career writing and performing as a member of the poetry collective 'The Mouthy Poets' and has gone on to perform her work both nationally and internationally. Georgina has featured at events such as the Edinburgh Fringe Festival, International Poetry Day: Granada, Sofar Sounds, Bright Spark, Hit the Ode, Straatstheatre Braunschweig and Off Milosz festival in Poland. As well as this, she has been commissioned by organisations such as The Royal Shakespeare Company, The Poetry Takeaway and BBC Radio Nottingham to write and perform, and has been invited to teach poetry for programmes such as the City Arts Refugee Forum collaboration, First Story, the National Literacy Trust, and Redhill Academy's specialisms week.

In 2019 Georgina was awarded a place on the prestigious Krakow City of Literature residency programme, and in the same year was commended as one of the Nottingham 30 under 30 winners for her work in poetry.

She has been published in literary journals such as *The Rialto* and *Kontent*, in magazines such as *Pussy Magic*, *Rebelotte* and *Left Lion*, and in anthologies such as Peace Builders *Small Acts of Kindness* and Jubilee Press' *The 'Aart of Nottingham*. In 2020 Georgina was invited to the Apples and Snakes BlackBox series to contribute her work 'Becoming a Street Lamp', and was also invited to write a piece on the Coronavirus pandemic for Manchester Writing School's Write We Are Now project in the same year.

She is incredibly proud to announce the release of her debut poetry collection, *Hag Stone*, out with Verve Poetry Press in 2022, as well as her recent long-listing in the OutSpoken prize for poetry performance category.

www.georginawildingpoet.co.uk
twitter: @WildingGeorgina

PRAISE FOR HAG STONE

'A debut collection of exuberant, sad, funny, clever poems, many of which are likewise succinct and intriguing. They cover a wide range of subjects with a wide range of techniques, moving between realism and surrealism to make their point. While the range of subjects and imagery is varied, and often unexpected or unpredictable, certain themes circle throughout the collection. There are poems about a difficult childhood, about humiliation, hatred, anger, aggression and sheer joie de vivre. Wilding's voice is distinctive, whether in softer, contemplative moments or full-on, head-on collisions with her inner and outer realities. This is definitely no boring read – indeed, as the irresistible opening line of 'Cod' declaims: 'What a luxury it is to be boring."

- **Jenny Swann**

'*Hag Stone* is a collection rooted in a stark urban world of 'sunken trollies and dropped dummies', of local parks and plastic dolls' houses, which, in this poet's hands, frequently becomes transcendent; a landscape where 'the last burning butts of a million cigarettes' become 'fallen stars we're standing on in trainers' or where 'Origami swans from Rizlas walk the park.' Recurring images and objects give a sense of searching and of an underlying menace at the edge of things. Georgina's poems about childhood and the traumas of young adulthood are particularly powerful, and at times, in poems such as Perspectives and July, pack a heart-stopping punch.'

- **Cathy Grindrod**

'You might think you already know this poetry but you are wrong. These carefully chosen images are filtered through an individual mind rich with experience and craft. The use of language is deft and endlessly engaging. This is a somewhat dark adventure through a world where the view from the other side of the known surprises, intrigues and often disturbs. This is poetry with intent to jar your perspective and bares reading slowly and again in silence so you can experience a world of other and look back on your own reality and reflect.' - **Henry Normal**

'In Georgina Wilding's tender first book, imagination has a violent power for those forced to grow up in the shadows. A spinning dolls house becomes a tornado, pulling a speaker inside. A young woman dehumanized by those around her thrashes among sunken trollies in a pond, 'asking for directions / back up to the surface of things.' This darkness, however, also intensifies the hard-won delight elsewhere at astral travel to Butlins and the ability to transform into streetlamps, bushes, meals. A flock of quick-winged surprises await discovery in the corners of this passionate, dynamic debut.' - **John McCullough**

'If I read this book without knowing Georgina Wilding was English, I would think these were translations from the daughter of Vasko Popa. Wilding has penned a book of sly surreal poems full of razored wit and tone shifts, a speaker who, Alice-like, shifts in size and age, trembling and tarrying in a world of gendered ironies, where hammerhead sharks are invited for tea, and red ants eat and regurgitate daughters. But despite their surreal turns, these are poems situated firmly in a brutal gendered world, with pills that take away children, where the fat girl drags you by the hair, where 'Boys beat you until you wet on the stairs like a dog,' where even the hours are 'small,' and we travel from dingy bars and uncles rolling joints, to find where a dead bee dies 'So much pollen/dusted its body/ it must've crashed/ through a net of stars/ just to land there.' For in the end,amidst the violence, there is more than can be held of beauty here. These are defiant poems, whose speakers are 'Never on our knees, begging the moon.' These are poems that will latch onto you like how 'koi mouth cunt,' and never let go. These are poems that 'refuse to come home.' - **Sean Thomas**

Georgina Wilding
Hag Stone

Ian ♥

I hope you find something
in here that speaks to you ♥
and hope to see you in the real
world soon!

A big tea-cheers to you!

Georgina
xxx

VERVE
POETRY PRESS
BIRMINGHAM

PUBLISHED BY VERVE POETRY PRESS
https://vervepoetrypress.com
mail@vervepoetrypress.com

FIRST PUBLISHED MAY 2022

Printed and bound in the UK
by ImprintDigital, Exeter

ISBN: 978-1-913917-10-4

Cover illustration: Emily Catherine Illustration
Cover design: Jamie Cole Design, Dean Wilkinson

Item: Hag Stone

A hag stone is a stone with a naturally occurring hole running through it, usually found in streams, rivers, or at the seashore. They're considered a talisman for many reasons, but in particular, due to their ability to gift anyone who peers through the hole The Sight; the ability to see the supernatural at work all around us.

Should you fall victim to relentless bad luck, illness and or general misfortune, it's likely a spell has been placed on you, someone around you, or something that you've recently brought into the home. Peering through a hag stone will reveal the malevolence at hand, and allow you to treat, defeat, or accept it, accordingly.

CONTENTS

'When I eventually did come round, I felt so much heavier. None of my limbs were where I thought they would be. Everything was a few inches out.' -

Abi Palmer, *Sanatorium*

Hag Stone

i

Rat

Fertile female rats can have up to 15,000 babies
a year, complaining about one seems futile.
Still, we call the exterminator,
write the cheque, and watch from the lounge.

As if sprinkling salt,
he leaves poisonous pellets in its lunch box,
slides snapping traps under its pillow,
and smears glue to the base of all its shoes.

If it leaves, he tells us, block up
all the entry points. This will get rid of the rat
by making it difficult for them
to enter their home or structure.

Still, it taunts us. A small thing, really,
wisp of its mother, curled
over the keyboard, school tie still on.
Each tap like a scratching
at the base of a barn door.

Suitcase

The case was black, trimmed with red piping,
and big enough to carry a weekend.
Regardless of the room,
it was always unzipping itself.

In the kitchen it rolled out, gawking
in front of the table as I ate,
the flap of its opening a mouth
trying to form the words.

I would sit in the hall by the door,
press my face against the glass and watch it fog.
As each breath cleared
I'd pray to see his silver car.

Sometimes it took 692 breaths
before my mum appeared with the phone.

The walks back through the living room to unpack
were the worst walks of shame I have ever known;
my father, uninterested, step father, gloating.

At night the case slept under my bed.
When dreaming it'd spin its wheels as if rolling,
and I could tell a nightmare from the pace.

By morning, it was out again, stood
on its four round feet,
zip wide open,
calling me in to be held.

Perspectives

I cannot pretend to know what was going
through his mind for the time that I lived there,
only that I was female and not his.

He would taunt me about the size of my ears,
my absent Dad. I would lock myself in the bathroom,
spit in his tea, cut buttons from his work shirts -
anything to gain some power back from the six foot man
with kicking feet and big voice.

My mother would coax him to lay on her lap, stroke
his black hair and expanse of shining forehead.
It was the ultimate maddening of me.

He told me I was difficult, pretty
like the Swedish girls, but with a face
like a slapped arse. I could do nothing
but boil in my own skin, and drink,
and scratch his car with stones,
and fall asleep in his house,
counting buttons instead of sheep.

A Scrap

Hanging there from his arms like a scrap
of universe hacked out and flaunted for trophy,
I suddenly became rough as an un-brushed tongue,
and when dropped, I was not soft, but sounded like the sickly
pat of a new-born lamb as it falls, embarrassed from its mother
and rolls, mottled, into the grass.

Ants

This is a garden with a plastic doll house full
of snails. Her chubby hands hold them like pebbles,
trace the spiral of their shells as if a map to the exit.

There's a seesaw, but one side's resting
in an ants nest. Before long the red biters
are up and over her jelly sandals. They cut skin
and spray acid in the wounds as they work their way up.

The neighbours hear the screams before anyone else.
Blindly batting at her body, bright and pocked,
pieces of her are ripped off and carried to the colony until,

in the long grass, a pair of jelly sandals rest empty.
The mother spends two weeks with a glass held from her ear
to the lawn and a copy of 'Understanding Ants',

becomes addicted to the smell of rain
and listening to the sound of them regurgitating
her daughter for their young.

Spider

A spider comes into my room - one so big it might walk up the stairs to my dollhouse, switch on the lights, and start an affair with the wooden doll's mother. It's fast, dresses well, and I can already see her peering from her wooden seat towards it. I try to kill it with a golf club before it makes the stairs, but he runs around the back and it's like the house has got legs and is turning itself around to let him in. So I snap the legs with the club, but two more grow in their place, and now the house is spinning itself in circles, and the spider is having second thoughts so I think, *let's keep this up*, and set the place on fire. I smash the cars in the drive and the wind picks up, and now the house is a tornado that's pulled the whole lot of us inside, and the spider and I are slapped into each other over and over, and I worry about his big legs, and his big fists, and the wooden mother has cracked down the middle and given him his own cereal, and I keep seeing half of her flung past the both of us, and I keep wondering if this was his plan all along.

Understanding Boys

We find condoms on Dad's bedside
and it's how we know
he's a boy. Boys stroke girls'
arms and ask them to kiss.
Boys only sometimes
show up when they say they will.
Boys have jobs. Boys ask you to get in
your pyjamas because jeans are too thick.
Boys are kind when they feel bad, boys are allowed
to smash things in temper. Boys tell you they know
how to brush your hair and don't get in trouble
when it has to be cut out. Boys follow
you to school and grab you in the alley.
Boys are husbands. Boys beat you until you wet
on the stairs like a dog. Boys recommend each other
on LinkedIn. Boys spend money they owe
your grandad. Boys think you can't
trick them. Boys eat girls
and deny it, drive cars with their knee caps,
turn the wheel with one hand. Boys get rabies
if you make them have veg. Boys get memory loss
if their phone brightness is up. Boys can't swim
in salt water unless it's their own. Boys are nose blind.
Boys hair is made from office lint. Boys brains
are made of microwave meals. Boys lose
one inch of height every time they say I love you.

The Upturned

We live underneath the armchair.
Turned on its front, it is the open mouth of a cave.

There's a rock pool inside, which is convenient
because we often invite hammerhead sharks for tea.

As the evenings crawl in you start up the fire,
I make smoke signals that bellow out
to some place called 'living room'
and we laugh about the mushroom on your belly.

Together we fall asleep in the heat and I dream-smell
the sawdust on your clothes, your skin.

Today, this is 'living room'
and I'm staring at an upturned armchair.
I've examined it from each angle, but can't find the way back in.

So, I pull out a match, force light from a candle,
and signal you for directions.

The Orange Dollhouse

The roof is the happening spot.
Many romances come and go,
Barbie and the bear,
Ken and the swan.
Each morning, I check
for a paw moved, a dress changed,
hoping to witness the last moments
of a proposal sabotaged by my arrival.
Instead, the dolls inside rigor mortis
on the matchstick bed, splay out
in the MDF hall, slump over
on the kitchen counter. Surely
the swan had spronked off
her short legs and aimed
for carpet, or the bear had Ken
in the boot. I hold the scissors
to Barbie's blonde mess
if you don't blink
I'll do it.
Still, the only sounds in the orange
house are mine. I hold the mother
doll's arms out wide like a bear trap,
and push the daughter closer in
a quarter inch by the hour.

The Gate

I've seen Grandad taking his watch off.
His fingers grew too fat for his sovereign
ring years before, and now, his skin
is becoming loose. It seems he's on the road
to somewhere I'd rather he not go.

Last week, I went to visit, and as I passed
their bedroom, the smell of the open gate
greeted me. I stood still and felt it slip around
my body, see if I would fit.
I knew then it'd been sizing him
up for months.

I'd never smelt that in their house before -
only in the homes of old widowed women,
or care homes, or hospital wards, never here.

Since then his belly has flattened -
it's no washboard, but it is not
the beaming sun I remember.

He still won't wear blue jeans though,
and keeps asking for socks at Christmas.
I suppose it a matter of pride -
when he walks through the gate
there'll be no holes at his toes.

I only hope, after all this shedding,
he keeps the cardigan I gave him
in case the breeze on the other side
is chillier than we think.

Water

The tulips, sure as May,
arrived in silence.
Pushed each other up
through the compact
earth with a strength
gathered from the shit
that buried them.
Inside one, a bee, curled
on its back by the base
of the style. What a handsome
place to die. So much pollen
dusted its body
it must've crashed
through a net of stars just
to land there.
I cut the stem and took it
to the silvery brook;
the water held the flower
like a boat. As it moved through
the foam-lipped current,
the soft tension sealed the two
together, suctioned in a
kiss, and whipped them both away from me.

ii

July

I took my mother with me.
We sat thigh-to-thigh, she watched
as I tipped my head back,
dropped the first pill into my mouth.

When she fell pregnant with me,
they didn't want kids,
so they looked into giving me up, she said.

We sat on the bus out of town,
two hours to pass with no vomiting allowed.
I clutched the leaflet from the protestors
with the picture of my six-week-old baby on the front.

A Filthy Eclipse

You are hiding in the corner of a filthy bar
hunched in your hiccups and slurred words -

spine bent like a beanstalk
towards her, your blonde sun.

I am dancing, all of us girls a warbling chorus
peppered with ash and the not knowing.

The night, our mother, arms out,
ushers us away, deeper into the crowd.

Here, I am in love with my body,
run my hands down the velvet on my hips

and move to some invisible thing,
some force of joy –

until I see you eclipse into her
and I am set alight -

burnt to dust.
The dark sweeps me away into a plastic cup,

tips me outside with the rest of the elements,
where each spec of me is blown in its own direction.

The HCG Blood Test

*'When broadcaster Sandi Toksvig was studying anthropology at
university, one of her female professors held up a photograph of an
antler bone with 28 markings on it. "This," said the professor, "is
alleged to be man's first attempt at a calendar." Toksvig and her fellow
students looked at the bone in admiration. "Tell me," the professor
continued, "what man needs to know when 28 days have passed?."'*

In the waiting room
I wondered what it would be like to be emptied,
to hold three teaspoons of myself up to the light.

Through the tinge there's a car crashed into our house,
an auntie washing gum from my hair,
a boyfriend taking coke in the bath.

In a beat up shop by the train station
there's a box of photo slides,
small plastic squares framing a thin piece of film -

have the sun shine through that and there are moments,
transparent imprints of bridesmaids, a child
with their tatty bear, a wild spread of hillside even.

There's clarity in light. Sure as the blood in my vial,
sure as the earliest tallying of months - not man's first attempt
at a calendar, but woman's, twenty eight lines carved in bone.

Morning

I saw a small bird in my toilet bowl, once,
featherless and pink,
with dark black smudges for eyes
and I was concrete for a long while after.

Green Hour

Something so small as an hour
has arrived on my doorstep. As it happens,
each of us has one to choose from.
Some of them smell of flasked coffee
in dawn hands. Others, like the bitter evidence
of a bike ride in the short shadows of evening.
All of them take us somewhere green –
to the lawns where pansies black mouths open 'oh',
the square recreations of cut grass and goal posts,
or memorial sites of wreath and stone.
We wonder what we'd look to without parks,
what they might be after all this worship.
Like us, the green's had time to stop
and consider itself.

Family Tapestry

In the family tapestry the uncles roll joints
open mouthed singing songs about penny arcades.

All of us are circled round one lighter as if a campfire,
hearing stories, no doubt, of brothers sneaking off
with other mens' wives.

The women in the tapestry hold wide smiles and cup
the ears of their children, raise glasses toward the waiter
and toast to our aunties life.

If you look close enough you'll see the threads
woven together through the pints, the lighter, the cold hands,
one generations' stitch bringing in a new one below it.

My stitch might have been a daughter.
I might have had her there with me, felt her weight on my knee,
brushed a curl from her face as people talked around us.

Before I leave I reach into the tapestry, pull a lily
from the bouquet. At home, I take a vase
from the cupboard under the sink,
put the flower straight to water.

The wet threads mould first, a green tuft creeping
up the stem. By the time it meets the woollen petals
it's as though the lily had lived,
the rot proof of its ending.

Local

A middle-aged woman with paws tattooed on her tits goes to the garden centre. She hangs around the coi carp, watches them come to the surface and mouth 'cunt' at her. Before the elderly couple are close enough to see, she pulls one out of the water, holds it in her hands until it stops thrashing, until the only thing moving is its desperate opening: 'cunt, cunt, cu'

ACE: The Adverse Childhood Experiences Study

At the table one of my arms was leaking,
the elbow, dry as dust,
but the crease, a valley-stream with a current of its own.

I dipped a finger in and stirred the reeds
which in turn brought the fish. I tore bread for them,
paid extra when the bill came to account for their portion.

Birds took refuge in the stream, dipping in
and shaking out their bodies like cabasas.
They left behind seeds from their feed
and grassland grew the length of my forearm
with ferns and foxgloves for the bees.

By morning so much time had passed
that small humans were beginning
to emerge from the water.
Some so fresh their gills remained.

I asked them, politely, to form a line.
One pushes an earring through the ridge of her nose.
Another tries to wiggle webbed toes in his socks.
A tiny queue forms across the table,
I lean in for a closer look - if they're to come
from me, there must be questions...
Yes or no:

Did a parent or other adult in the water often or very often...
swear at you, insult you, put you down, or humiliate you?

Did a parent or other adult in the water often or very often...
push, grab, slap, or throw something at you?

Did you often or very often feel that ...
no one in your family loved you or thought you were important?

Did you often or very often feel that ...
you didn't have enough to eat, and had no one to protect you?

Recreation Ground

Every Friday we'd drink Vodka.
In the wet grass the boys would ask the girls to get-off.
We'd display our best MTV-tongues-out-hand-in-hair-kisses.

When asked if we'd ever do-more
the circle of girls pulled back in succession,
rolled eyes, shook heads. Jan and I quickly
followed, tripping, brushing off the nights
we would hide behind my bed,
her on the floor, me on top,
and rub together.

We married men in the field,
wore bottle cap rings to prove our dedication
and friends threw corner shop crisps for confetti.
We busied ourselves by organising dandelions
into neat rows and when the husbands built sheds
we made sure they were polished.
We even had children, dipped their heads
in adjacent puddles as Christening, and taught them
to count by picking chestnuts.

What wives we were.
Never sneaking to the graveyard behind the birches.
Never stopping to taste the sweat on each other's skin.
Never on our knees, begging the moon.

On the 152 four boys sit together

tut their tongues and bat their hands miming ping pong.
As the mouth-tutting-paddle-bats get louder,
one of the boys stares intently at the other's mouth.
Maybe to check that the serve is legal,
or, maybe to watch the 'o' of his lips as he makes the sound
and wonder if he might slip inside it.

On Duty

Oh, a spider,
great. Hope you didn't lay eggs
on me. What would I even do
with those? I couldn't fry them or
bake them or slosh them up
and drink them, or sell them
at the market wearing moccasins, or
put them on the drive
with a 'free eggs' sign and I certainly
couldn't raise them
as my own, what kind of father
do you think I am?

Granny Pants

It happened bent over the desk in DT
reaching for a nail,
when her shirt came untucked,
knickers gathered baggy over the waistband
like the white warning of the under
fluff of a rabbits' tail.

The boys' necks turned so quick
they snapped, became a forest of crooked trees
for the others to creep
behind and hunt for the big granny
pants on the tiny girl-body.

The rest of us scattered,
jumped from windows, ran
for the corridors. The astroturf
couldn't stop them digging through,
and the groundsman spent two weeks
trying to fill the holes back up.

My group had a warren
behind the bike shed.
Things ran smooth
enough down there.
Every so often
one of us would bungee ourselves
into a thong, walk the lines
of the football pitch,
elastic up over our chub,
and try to use the shadows
from the sun to track the time.

Vitamin D

There's something already in our skin,
some prohormone that waits for sun
to stamp its ticket and send it around the body.

It moves through the bloodstream, liver, kidney,
and eventually stands in our bones,
fortifying us like museums with scaffolds and grout.

I've been offering cheap entry fees to small people,
have hired a tour guide who shows them around my inside,
talks through my artefacts

and apologises for sections closed off for refurbishment -
there's not been much sun of late
but no one seems to mind.

According to reviews,
my chipped tooth is a thing of beauty
from the inside, the jagged roof,
like cut crystal, shatters the light and people
love to dance in it.

There's been requests for weddings in that tooth,
but I'm hesitant to host a party I can't technically attend,
and how would I explain the music playing
every time I opened my mouth?

At closing time, some of the people stay,
sneak into corners or wrap themselves under folds of skin
until the lights go out and it's safe to reappear.

Of course I don't tell on them,
Instead I lay awake, watch them graffiti
the inside of my eyelids
and wince as they eat
wafts of my organs like jam.

After It

Some of us cry about our mothers,
then spritz another layer of Charlie Red.
We spin into a paste on the roundabout,
drip from the seats into stalactites,
which the others snap off and eat like Skegness rock.

Empty cans thrown overhead are rockets
we try to straddle, but miss.
Instead, we straddle our lovers– in bushes,
up banks, in cars –

curled over the steering wheel, or a bench, or a bin.
We hold ourselves up,
spread our cheeks and let the boys in –
wet with the stickiness of the day and nothing else.

The mud of the football field is littered with
the last burning butts of a million cigarettes.
It's as if all the stars have fallen
and we're standing on them in trainers.

Each of us bear things –
me, a grudge against the boy
who promised me
the condom in his sock
but later stretched it over his head,
blew it up through his nostrils.

Now he's floated to the telephone lines
and there's a crowd balanced
on each other's shoulders to pull him back down.

Origami swans folded from Rizzlas walk the park.
We have the boys piss in a nearby ditch
so they have a pond to swim in,
and admire the things we can bring to life.

The night backs away from us,
turns its face as the last cigarette burns out.
We threaten *please don't go, I'll eat you whole,*
and scramble towards the black.

The field blooms with crawling girls,
knees caked in ash and mud,
reaching for the corners of the night's coat.
Some of them think they've found a pocket,
climb inside and promise to sleep.

Others use hair grips to stab it down in its tracks,
pin it to the soil, spread it out like a tent floor.
The crying starts, echos bounce between the trees –

the coat slips to a single thread across the horizon,
the hard slap of morning shuts our mouths.

Sent

I want to write poems with four legs that can carry themselves down the M1, slipping under cars and wedging their corners between the pipes to hitch a ride and get to you quicker. I want to write poems with four legs and a brain, sniffing out that tube air smell to follow, so, poems with four legs and a brain and a nose. They sniff from street to street, fold themselves up to slip through your letterbox, climb the stairs and know which room is yours because they've found the trainers that perfectly shape around your feet by the door, and they come in, and they sit, and they hold their tail (they have a tail now) and they howl at you from the end of the bed, and they howl at you from the end of the bed, and they howl at you from the end of the bed, and you wake up, and you look at their eyes, and they fold themselves flat again, onto your lap, and you hold them, and you pet them, and they won't come home.

2003-2004

Past the park where the fat girl drags you
by your hair and leaves you at your stepfather's feet.

Past the high street with the Asda guard
who'll let you in to piss so long as you act sober.

Past the place you work where the old man complains you're a slag
even though you're in a fleece and it's just red lipstick.

Past the jitty with your man who feeds a Smartie to a fox
with as much care as when he slips a penknife in your pussy.

Past the McDonalds where the boy in purple is stabbed to death
and only the kids with mopeds can put a face to the name.

Past the waters edge where the councilmen scrape dead rats
from their traps and drop them into the bags they drape over their
        shoulders.

You are drawing your mother on the pond scum with a stick;
you lurch for her throat.

You are thrashing towards the bottom
of all the sunken trollies and dropped dummies.

You are asking for directions
back up to the surface of things.

iii

Skin

A berry throws itself from a great height.
Splits its skin on the pavement below as if opening
its coat. As if asking the finches to look
at it while it points at the bruises
and the mold growing inside.

The birds gather round,
their brown shirts buttoned to the collar,
ties tucked in to avoid the mess.

Each bird scrapes the pulp from the berry, its juice
stains the yellow of their beaks like lipstick.

All that's left is the coat,
scarlet red and strewn at their feet.
Each set of beaded eyes stare down at it -
bloated bodies shift their weight.

Above, the surviving berries gather themselves,
pray for rain to wash the coat away
and start painting their bodies blue.

The Second Floor

Whilst she screamed at him for not turning up,
kettle whistling her words through gritted teeth,
the two above are moving furniture -
a constant rearrangement, thundering jolts.

And below, the two in the kitchen shout
ingredients, one dutifully emptying the fridge
while the other draws faces in the burning bacon.

As he comes back with grudges
he's been sharpening for weeks,
the sound of sliced air mutes the upstairs furniture.
The pair hide inside their newly placed wardrobes,
with the un-ironed clothes wrapped around their ears
in preparation for the bellowing. But it does not come.

Instead, it is wet, and as the screaming room fills to ceiling
with tears, and the floorboards in the room above swell
out of place, and the wardrobes are boats now.

The smoke below is flattened to coat the kitchen floor,
as the water runs out through the light fixtures
and the two make rafts of pots and pans.

And as the staircase fills, and the corridor fills, and
the rooms and rooms fill, paper wrinkles on all the walls,
and the logs from the fire bob up from their bed,
and the cat tries a doggy paddle, and the door is pushed off,
the wave-machine-sobs, a tide, and the whole house is drained.

And the crying, grudging two cascade,
gasping for air through the rooms of the house,
out onto the pavement, where the others float
on matching furniture and pans tied together with tea towels.

Dying Off

From germination to growth to flower
to seed, I use the lupin
to track when I died,
she tells me each time i'll come back
other. I haven't seen myself
in weeks, is this below ground?
The people here convince me it's not
worms on their skin. To the lupin,
i'm other. Each night I grab
for something still. *Sir, that is a worm.*
This keeps happening to me. I grab
for something, but haven't seen myself
in weeks, is this below ground? This keeps
happening to me, from germination to
growth to flower to seed.

On Parenthood

Before you climb, find a circle of 8 hazel branches. Push them into the ground, anchoring them securely. Dig in a barrow load of organic sweet, retain water and gently feed the hungry, flowering season is in the newspaper. A foot-wide strip of washed sand is great for growing smaller scale young. Tie them into the frame, don't leave them to flop around. Once a fortnight they start to romp away. Let them get on with it and pick pick pick as they're growing.

Mirrors

When you fall asleep, your astral body leaves your actual body and travels to places like Butlins. It gets sugar high on candyfloss and races all the other astrals on the go-karts, throws up over the barrier still wearing its helmet, and ends the trip at a magic show making a mockery of the magician and his glitter and string. On a usual night, when the astral returns, it lowers itself back into you like you're an incredibly narrow bath, and gets to work giving you dreams. On the nights you forget to cover the mirrors, it's startled by its naked reflection, all wisp and grey, dipping back into you, and chucks about nightmares in temper. Worse still, it confuses its reflection in the mirror with the actual body, tries to enter with a head-butt and lays unconscious on the carpet for days at a time. I stepped over mine this morning, felt a draft across my feet and haven't been able to tolerate all the bright and intact people since.

Cherry Tree

The cherry tree in the garden is pushing
out tiny pink fists; It's an effort to demonstrate
false strength, its sugared petals mottle in simple rain.

On warmer days I watch the aphids pierce its bark,
I spray the lupins, fox gloves, roses,
keep the bugs off the jasmine, acer, iris,
the tree holds me in contempt.

April ends and with its departure the cherry unclenches,
I resent the way time makes it softer.
For two weeks a year it's daughter-pink and ruffled,
for two weeks a year it does its job -

catches me off guard like a neighbour at the gate.
I watch myself with the Weedol, first sight of something
wrong and the whole lawn is poisoned,
I don't want to go on soaking it up.

Alarm

The house behind us has been crying for weeks.
The terraces budged closer in to prop it up,
and the birds stopped nesting out of respect.

It's a wailing sound, stuck on loop.
All its windows are smashed from the pressure,
its plants up past the chimney from the tears.

There's no real sight of the house at all,
just swamp oozing out to the road
and no one's got Sky because the electricity lines
have snapped in the canopies.

None of us can sleep until our own terraces straighten
themselves up again, beds no longer at an angle,
but even with the trees gone and windows boarded
there's still the flooding and the wailing.

The teenage girls brought pyjamas and organised a sleepover
to address the situation, asking if it's ok
and wants to talk, but some of them drowned in the night
now all communication has been banned.

So here we are, everyone in wellies and earmuffs floating their kids
to school in plastic boxes and shouting MORNING, HOW ARE YOU?
GOOD THANKS HOW ARE YOU? and sleeping standing up.

Boulder

In a recurring dream I'm digging the borders,
my body clenched to the ground,
and with every shovel I lift,
the mud fills back in.

On my knees, I use my hands to push the earth.
From behind, I look like a boulder.
I want to drop off the edge of this day and flatten
whatever's at the bottom - a village, a child -
but a single crocus pushes back at me,
furiously upright, like a bitter mother's finger signing no.

Proposal

I have fallen in rogg with you,
crestboot girl,
dremarien girl,
as you kneel on London Bridge
tiny chewing-gum.
Below the boats are wepling by,
open mouthed,
and I am Poseidon
jewel encrusted
rising a spinning wet from the water
walloping all into the grey-scape glom
sending wild horses from the waves
up through the coblets
and the sky is mimicking -
chucking hailstones -
peoples heads splitting open like clams
my arms up in the shape of a 'y'
like a wine glass and you pour
your whole skaxis into me
and I yoffa you up
tiny skizzle
wet bronea
thine.

Cod

What a luxury it is to be boring,
to sit on wooden show chairs as unenthused as the cod;
slapped across the cheek with ice and propped dead
behind the supermarket glass.

To see no need to smile or speak with music,
just a sound like a boat engine driving out the mouth -
perhaps some faint memory of the catch.

Slumped in grey and flaking,
no one asks where the iridescent scales are, the high shine,
instead they hail that fish as the nation's favourite
and serve it up, spineless, every Friday night.

Pain

It has to be mustard,
as if a thousand cracked seeds were sewn together,
strong and bitter, and melted into velvet.
Like a paste smeared over me, its folds, a gathering
where the knife has turned in its spread.

It will cinch me in,
I'll become a tall wasp, spare legs tucked in the pockets,
wings humming below the collar.
Like, at any turn, I could sting –
small children, men in shorts - and survive.

Becoming a Street Lamp

I stood on the pavement,
up close to someone's wall
and became a street lamp.

It wasn't difficult,
I outstretched both my arms,
held a cigarette by the tip of its butt,
stood on my toes and willed it so.

That's when I learnt I could will things.
Before long I could rustle like any good bush,
so convincing small bugs would cocoon on my leaves
and dogs would run past without sniffing me out.

I was proudest when I learnt to be a meal,
would watch men eat chunks of me and think
how nutritious I am, how satisfying.
Prouder still when I learnt I could choke them
on the way down.

I could be the coffin they were buried in, too,
cradle them softly in the mud and then slip out,
let them lay there, naked as the day they laid with me.

An Auntie at a Birthday Party

That night I counted the seconds
between each flash of disposable camera
to see how close the storm was.

Around tables, girls discussed the boys
fist pumping on the dance floor -
decided it was him, on the left,
most suitable for 'the look.'

They shared the same
Mac chilli gloss, popped their lips,
blotted the excess with napkins
and admired the petals of the prints left over.

One picked up a cardboard tie,
held it to her collarbone
and invited the boy into her selfie.

Seconds past the flash,
another boy appeared an
slapped the camera from their faces.

Amidst the rutting of bodies,
spilt drinks, and squealing
trainers on the vinyl,
came a woman.
She wrapped her hand
around his tall throat.

In that grip I saw
all the doors she'd locked,
and the way she left the key in, half turned,
so it couldn't be undone from the outside.
I saw the radio she'd leave playing at night,
it's voices standing guard in the hall.

I saw her little girl,
how she taught her
to recognise the '9'
on the keypad of the phone.

By the time her hand re-opened,
he was standing upright in the middle of it
smaller than all of us,
walking the lines of her palm.

Every girl in that bar, camera flashes
casting light-shadows on their faces,
looked from the woman's hand
to their own, and back again.

ACKNOWLEDGEMENTS

Thank you to these organisations for facilitating the creation of these poems and the opportunity to further develop as a writer:

Arts Council England
Nottingham UNESCO City of Literature
Krakow UNESCO City of Literature / Villa Decius
Apples and Snakes
New Writing North
Writing East Midlands
The Arvon Foundation
The University of Nottingham
The Mouthy Poets

Thank you to these organisations for publishing early drafts or commissioning some of the poems featured in this book:

The Rialto
Apples and Snakes / The Royal Shakespeare Company
Kontent Magazine (KRK)
Pussy Magic digital magazine
Write we are Now / Manchester Metropolitan University
Left Lion Magazine
Rebelotte Press
Nottingham Peacebuilders
Nottingham Poetry Festival

THANKYOUS

Thank you to Leanne and Josh for all the early poems they read, and for keeping me brave. Thank you to Emily, who held me steady through the writing of this book. Thank you to my mentors, Caroline Bird and Andrew McMillan, for conjuring these poems out of me, and Caroline, for all the hours with the manuscript. Thank you to Stuart, for giving this book a home. Thank you to Danny, for being my home. Thank you to my aunties, for their consistent outpouring of love. And to my Grandparents, for everything.

ABOUT VERVE POETRY PRESS

Verve Poetry Press is a quite new and already prize-winning press that focused initially on meeting a local need in Birmingham - a need for the vibrant poetry scene here in Brum to find a way to present itself to the poetry world via publication. Co-founded by Stuart Bartholomew and Amerah Saleh, it now publishes poets from all corners of the UK - poets that speak to the city's varied and energetic qualities and will contribute to its many poetic stories.

Added to this is a colourful pamphlet series, many featuring poets who have performed at our sister festival - and a poetry show series which captures the magic of longer poetry performance pieces by festival alumni such as Polarbear, Matt Abbott and Imogen Stirling.

The press has been voted Most Innovative Publisher at the Saboteur Awards, and has won the Publisher's Award for Poetry Pamphlets at the Michael Marks Awards.

Like the festival, we strive to think about poetry in inclusive ways and embrace the multiplicity of approaches towards this glorious art.

www.vervepoetrypress.com
@VervePoetryPres
mail@vervepoetrypress.com